HARM'S WAY

HARM'S WAY

POEMS BY ERIC LEIGH

The University of Arkansas Press
Fayetteville
2010

Copyright © 2010 by The University of Arkansas Press

All rights reserved
Manufactured in the United States of America

ISBN-10: 1-55728-930-1
ISBN-13: 978-1-55728-930-8

14 13 12 11 10   5 4 3 2 1

Designed by Liz Lester

♾ The paper used in this publication meets the minimum requirements of the American National Standard for Permanence of Paper for Printed Library Materials Z39.48-1984.

LIBRARY OF CONGRESS CATALOGING-IN-PUBLICATION DATA

Leigh, Eric, 1973–
    Harm's way : poems / by Eric Leigh.
        p.   cm.
    ISBN-13: 978-1-55728-930-8 (pbk. : alk. paper)
    ISBN-10: 1-55728-930-1 (pbk. : alk. paper)
    I. Title.
    PS3612.E3565H37   2010
    811'.6—dc22
                            2009052400

For my mother,
Judy Mae Schultz

And in memory of my father,
Leo Calvin Breedon

ACKNOWLEDGMENTS

Grateful acknowledgement is made to the editors of those publications in which the following poems originally appeared, sometimes in earlier versions.

Cimarron Review: "On the Day the Last Drag Queen Leaves Town"
The Gay & Lesbian Review Worldwide: "Origami Heart"
Good Foot Magazine: "The Last Remains of the Country Heart"
Lifeboat: "Loving the Haberdasher"
MARGIE: The American Journal of Poetry: "At The Rhinestone Bullet"
The Nation: "Harm's Way"
New England Review: "My Mother Reads Tobacco Road," "Results"
New Letters & Poetry Daily: "The Dark-Light of Spring"
Passages North: "Country Letter"
The Princeton Arts Review: "Skilled Trades" (under a different title)
Salt Hill: "Letter, January"
West Branch: "Hymn," "Catching a Stranger's Eye during the Changing of the Guard"
Zone 3: "Oh, Loretta," "On the Line," "Bystander Effect"
"Last of the Midnight Lullabies" appeared in the anthology *Next to Godliness: Finding the Sacred in Housekeeping* edited by Alice Peck.
"Juleps" appeared in the anthology *This New Breed: Gents, Bad Boys, and Barbarians Volume 2* edited by Rudy Kikel.

Many thanks to the wonderful staff at the University of Arkansas Press, especially Enid Shomer.

My sincerest gratitude to the MFA Program in Creative Writing and the Hopwood Awards Program at the University of Michigan, the Stadler Center for Poetry at Bucknell University, *The Nation* magazine and the 92nd Street Y, the Robison Jeffers Tor House Foundation, and the Dorothy Sargent Rosenberg Awards for their generous support. A special thanks to the family members, friends, teachers, and others who have championed me and my work over the years, including but not limited to Michael Abdou, Crystal Allen, Geoffrey Breedon, Matthew Carrigan, Gabrielle Civil, Ross Chambers, Rick Dutra, Toby Dyner, Alison Fletcher, Alice Fulton, Linda Gregerson, Lizzie Hutton, Eric Kessell, Cynthia Kolanowski, Simon Craddock Lee, Marc W. Lester, Brandi Lewis-Lail, Arnulfo Lopez, Thylias Moss, Drew Nolan, Ernie Ortiz, Saul Palomera, Robert Portilla, James Richardson, Elliot Ruchowitz-Roberts, Grace Schulman, Keith Schultz, Renée Sedliar, Laura Sutherland, Kim Yaged, and Frank Yamrus.

CONTENTS

I.

Homesong 3

Skilled Trades 4

My Mother Reads Tobacco Road 6

Last of the Midnight Lullabies 7

Juleps 9

Bystander Effect 10

Life in the Rearview Mirror 11

On the Day the Last Drag Queen Leaves Town 12

The Controlled Burn of Carolina Dirt 14

Country Letter 15

On the Line 17

Oh, Loretta 19

The Last Remains of the Country Heart 20

Gun Country 22

The Dark-Light of Spring 23

II.

Bel Canto for Beginners 33

Hymn 34

Catching a Stranger's Eye during the
Changing of the Guard 36

Origami Heart 37

Loving the Haberdasher 38

Letter, January 39

At The Rhinestone Bullet   40

At This Late Hour   42

Understory   44

Earthquake Weather   45

Notes on Drowning   47

Assisted Living   48

For Those Who Cannot Make the Journey   50

Color Theory   51

Results   52

Harm's Way   53

Watching the Virus Attack a Cell   55

Sickness & Health   57

Notes   60

I.

Families will not be broken. Curse and expel them,
send their children wandering, drown them in floods and fires,
and old women will make songs out of all of these sorrows
and sit in the porches and sing them on mild evenings.

—MARILYNNE ROBINSON

Homesong

Another oil slick sky, another night
of the mercury light's electric hum
sounding high above the darkened fields
of my childhood, the old farmhouse empty
except for my brother and me.

Our father working third, mother sleeping single
in town, in the white stink of fresh paint.
I grab the flashlight and walk the dogs.
They run into bramble, and I wait for them
in the blue-hued spell of the lamp.

But they won't come back, lured away
by meat and marsh, another night of feeding,
the lamp revealing all of us. I lie down
in the expanse of what was my parents' bed.
Across the hall, I can hear my brother hunt

and peck the keys of Daddy's old electric,
typing a school report—the family tree branches
yet again. The dogs are barking their secrets
back and forth across the corn, but I know better
than to chase after them through the field

so green it must have eaten bones to get that color,
know how each rough husk reaches out
to touch you at this hour, grabs the denim
of your worn Levi's, welcomes your whole body
with the firm handshake of loss.

Skilled Trades

My father comes home with a six-pack
smile and stinking of oil. And this
is a promotion, something to celebrate.

I grill steaks, mash potatoes, choose red
instead of white, and start some laundry.
Now there'll be more of it—T-shirts, jeans,

white cotton socks—all stained with the bruises
of oil, lube that keeps the line chugging,
turning out transmissions so everyone can go

and he can come home wearing that blue-collar
cologne that fills this house. I do the wash
just like Mama would if she were here,

use the strongest shit you can buy to keep the oil
from ruining jeans. But you'll wreck yourself
trying to get the smell gone once it's got a home,

like my books he takes to work, my paperback
Leaves of Grass, beat up and smelling of him,
the oilcan scent of a man. Even Uncle Walt falls

under this industrial swoon, how we stain
the things we hold closest to our hearts.
He finds me folding colors. Still happy,

he shows me his finger smashed from some
machine, the nail gone black with trapped blood.
I heat a needle with his lighter, press the fired

metal through the nail until blood swells,
trying not to go too far, but still he whispers,
"It hurts." "It will," I say. And it does.

My Mother Reads Tobacco Road

Only thirteen and already a star
pupil in the school of hard knocks,
she cracks open the book to the day's

last lesson: someone else's misery
can quiet your own. Extra credit: a heart
has no avenues, just a puzzle

of dirt roads that snake for no reason.
She reads until the flashlight dies.
Tomorrow, another day of putting on

and taking off her mother's apron,
of gathering dandelion greens
and making a meal out of bitterness

to feed children who never get full
and always take her for the one who bore them
into this world, where each of them

will one day play the part
of that young girl Pearl—wedded too soon
to sorrow, hunger, a no-good man.

Not her, not ever, she tells herself
and sleeps. Years later, her marriage shot,
the house sold, she pulls down the book

just to throw it away. Some roads
don't need to be braved twice, a decision
born of fear, respect, or a little of both.

Last of the Midnight Lullabies

Middle of the night, my grandfather calls
stuck again in that foxhole,
his buddy's head shot straight off.

Or he thinks he's still in the asylum
where the only sounds he heard
were from the past—stray bullets,

his own sobs. Now, when he cries
my mother's name, he does so as if she were a child
in danger and he the father he never was.

In five minutes we're on our way
down the same back roads we drove years before,
taking my dad to his second-shift,

those graveyard hours I sat in the back,
my mother telling me to sleep. But there is no
going back to the peace of what was.

When we arrive, my mother kills the headlights
and begins doing what she does best.
There's no wrinkled sheet her hands can't smooth,

no ruined blouse or man she can't rescue
with club soda or her touch.
The truth lives just beneath her perfume:

hold a man long enough and eventually he'll cry—
hold him longer and he'll stop. We find him
on the couch in his tattered robe

and old-man slippers, empty bottle at his side.
"Warm him some milk," my mother says,
and I do what I'm told as she goes to him

and strokes his head, hums him that lullaby,
the one she made up out of his absence
and the nights her mother worked,

out of a need to calm herself and a farmhouse
full of children. Part of her is still that girl
in worn-through shoes, wandering

from room to room, checking the eyes
of every child to make sure they are sleeping.
Memory lane is a minefield of twice-learned lessons.

Consider this: it was an early frost like this one
when he plucked a fallen wasp nest from the ground
to help me kill my fear.

He peeled back the paper of a cell
and coaxed a worker from its bed.
Impossible still, the way the wasp crawled

up his thumb and threw itself to the wind,
how those moments we're woken from
stay with us and stay true.

When he's still, we cover him with blankets.
Maybe now he'll forget enough to fall asleep
as we stand at the kitchen sink, mining the space

between night and day, ritual and work.
I wash. She dries. We both look straight ahead,
cleaning up another mess and staring down the dawn.

Juleps

A few days before her forty-sixth birthday,
all my mother wants is to sip mint juleps
and sit on the porch.

She doesn't know what it is about this drink
except regret, never having tasted mint
swirling in bourbon,

so I break the ice with a quick twist of tray,
muddle leaves and jigger whiskey,
but there's only so much sugar—

not enough for more than two drinks,
not enough to cover coming out to my mother.
How much of this is useless subterfuge?

Mint doesn't hide the taste of Jim Beam
any better than I hide myself
as we raise our glasses in a toast

to the sweet sting of age, to the burn of julep
in the back of our throats, to the things we think
and the things we say aloud.

Bystander Effect

Her face hits my window and you slam the brakes
      as her body is flung to the side of the road

where we find her and are grateful for the lack of blood.
      You rush to her, while I stand here where I always stand,

left of center, just downstage in a December
      so stubborn and green that the geese have forgotten

to take leave, the deer continue to run. I hope
      she's stunned, that she'll jump to as I once saw happen.

Before we know it, a neighbor comes to see if we're okay,
      if we want to keep her, this doe made ours by impact.

It's cold, but we know the score. She must be cleaned,
      her belly cut before the blood settles, spoils the meat.

His boldness allows us the easy out of grieving.
      While he takes care of business, you kneel next to her,

stroke her fur, whispering something lost to air. Your words
      just steam, too little and too late. I should have seen

the signs sooner—the lone cardinal on the way out
      of the drive, the places in your heart I'll never know.

When I turn, I see how her coat has cleaned the door,
      what was covered with salt now shines a deep maroon.

Life in the Rearview Mirror

Last night, a busted lip
from the boys in town.
Now you're smiling
just to prove you still can,

fixing your face
with your mother's base,
while she does the wash
and the old man gets crocked.

The days are the same
but they are numbered.
Tonight, while others sleep
under the wool of the past,

you coast the car down the drive,
check your makeup in the rearview,
and accept one last gift
from the calloused hands of boys:

the mailbox hanging
from the side of its post,
little red flag on the side of the road,
one less reason to drop a line.

On the Day the Last Drag Queen Leaves Town

The boys downstairs huff gasoline
off strips of Mother's emerald gown,
making what joy they can
out of fume and a knockoff Halston.
No note, no explanation, only thing
she left is a hole where reason should be.
You grow a heart there and feed it leftovers:
stray earrings, scuffed-out pumps,
the soft pink flame of her first feather boa.
How it curled around her shoulders
when she did the lucky snake dance,
the one with the shimmy, where her hands
dangled at her side and slapped her hips.
And then she'd wave her hand across the air
just as she did every morning when
you'd wake her with an orange for breakfast,
a bowl of milk for her facial, and she'd give
you a word: *banana,* somehow transformed
by the dissonance of painted lips and baritone.
Truth is you'll be just fine. Remember, a girl
in high heels can still win a race.
You're just missing the way she knew you—
the way the tree stump loves the ax,
because the blade still sees a use in an old piece
of oak. Drive into town and get drunk,
watch the sole streetlight turn yellow,
sway in the breeze. Wait for someone to ask
about him, then testify. Tell them *she* was

last seen two-stepping into the dawn, working
the moon for its last bit of butter, the wig
slipping from her head. Because if somebody
goes asking about Mother, seems they need
a happy ending. Go ahead, give it.

The Controlled Burn of Carolina Dirt

Something is burning, but the wind won't say exactly what:
an old pile of tires, the whole damn countryside.
And when you pull in the drive, you know for sure
you'll always be too late to save anything or anyone
except for yourself. The house of your childhood is now just a frame
of char, and the sky through the burned-out roof is as clear as the truth
always should be. Your mother went default, and the local fire co.
bought the deed to use the place for practice. Even now, the house is only
a simulation, and somewhere she is waiting for you with a tumbler
full of ice and a thousand excuses. It's so you, the way you run
toward what is already gone, but the mirage of the past turns into sand
when the apprentice firemen catch you and, as only men can, keep you
safe, while also keeping you equidistant from exactly what you need.
You fall to your knees and plant yourself in the dirt just outside of what was
your front door, the same dirt that always found its way around your collar
and underneath your nails, the dirt your mother always swept under
the welcome mat, the cigarette in her mouth turning to ash.
Your hands pound that dirt a certain, secret number of times,
as if the past will open up. But the past is not a house you can enter
or a lock you can pick. The past is a flame you must learn to hold
your hand above, because no one, not even these men, can put it out
for good. It rises up in you, a series of heats: hot tears, flushed cheeks,
and the burn of your hands on that Carolina dirt, a rage your heart has known
and known again. This is love and what it can do. When one of the men
asks if you're all right, you answer in that voice from all those years ago:
"I'm fine. I'm okay." It's his answer that makes you stand.
"Even when the smoke dies, fires burn a few more days."

Country Letter

Darling, everything here is as I left it, just older
and worse for wear: the rusted flatbed I drive to town,
the bullet holes outside The Little Grass Shack
where years ago a man was shot to death.
The stain on the pavement still rises red
with the first drop of rain and it's coming—a good end
to August's last stand, this heat that burns the yard yellow
and slows the old man's breath, makes him dizzy.

I give him cold baths in the evening,
and the doctor says *any time,*
and the blood on the sidewalk says
all we thought was gone is still with us
or on its way back. Reason enough to stay up
all night and think about how if you were here
we'd go walking past the slanting ruin
of the hog house, past the old transistor
crackling Pasty Cline across the corn.

I'd show you the hayloft
where I first kissed a boy, his lips
making static against mine, a small fire burning
where no one could see. He smelled like the marsh
smells right now—the fallen trees turning to mulch,
the leaves to soil.

This quiet drives me crazy.
I turn on the TV, the radio, anything
for noise. I've gone so far as to hang wind chimes
on the back porch and ask the night to play me

something you'd play if I were home,
your hands like lightning over the ivory.

Last night, I found him crying at the window
and tried to put him back to bed, but he pulled away.
Then I saw them through the glass: the deer
in the garden, two does eating tulips from the flower bed,
chewing the petals down to soft, green stems.
They came right up to the house, had nothing
to be afraid of. How I want the same for us.

On the Line

The union steward calls at the crack of dawn, sorry
to bother us, but he wants my brother and me to know
the sooner we pick up our father's things, the better.
"Sometimes on the line," he says and hesitates,

"things can disappear." I want to say I know.
After all, how many times was my father's job
or his love resting on that very line—
a place where the best things sit at risk.

It's been two days since he did himself in,
and here I am in the shit-hole that wrecked his knees
and back with twenty years of machine repair.
The steward meets us with a firm handshake

and his name: Sterling—a bad joke
on any day, today made worse by circumstance.
I don the required safety glasses and do my best
to follow as he leads us to the storage room,

where he unlocks the door and I sign to take possession.
But the tool chest is too heavy for my brother and me
to lift into our borrowed flatbed, so together
the three of us roll the old gal down the line.

As we pass their stations, the men each nod,
tug the rim of their hard hats in a welcome that's a bit

too nice, as if they've seen the coroner's chicken scratch:
self-inflicted gunshot wound to chest.

A few of them come to offer the condolence
of brute force, help us heft the tools into the truck.
And just then, as we shoulder the weight, I see
that these good old boys, these carbon copies of my dad

with their rough hands and dirty jokes, are beautiful.
When we're done, Sterling pulls us aside
and slides us a union check cut by his own hand.
"This is for you, boys. I know it's not much."

We've got my father's Buick and his mortgage,
a box of tools we cannot use, and a check
for a hundred bucks. When I go to give the glasses back,
Sterling waves his hand and smiles, "Yours to keep."

Oh, Loretta

It's all over but the crying, promises the jukebox.
Another Saturday night, another nowhere along the banks
of the Susquehanna, waiting for a drink strong enough to quiet
my dead father. He insists on this beer hall, on Bushmill's
by the glass, and on quarters for the second-rate Wurlitzer.
We wait our turn in the queue until the slide guitar of her voice
comes on same as always. Same as same. There's always a tramp
about to steal her man, but he never leaves her side as she gives
birth to baby, song, or love. Maybe the child you get
is not the one you want but the one that kicks your ass.
That's enough, says my father. *I wanna go.* It's his idea
to take the long way, to cross the train bridge by foot.
I want to jump, but he arm-wrestles me for it and I lose.
Just like old times, he says and smiles. "It's not easy," I tell him.
"On my hands and knees, I cleaned your blood from the carpet."
Stop your bitching, he says. *Think about Loretta, only thirteen
and knocked up in the blue hills—Good Lord!* He slaps his thigh,
amuses himself as he's always done and points toward
the old, white barn on the other side of the river,
the one that was a stop on the underground railroad,
its fresh coat of paint almost ghostly at this hour.
He runs into that glowing white and I cannot follow,
only cry her song across the bank. Oh, Loretta,
daughter of the dark stuff, why'd he go? What's the use
in all this coal if you never make a diamond, cut some glass,
crawl through the window into a new life?

The Last Remains of the Country Heart

You only get one chance to scatter
your father's ashes, which are not even ash
if the truth be told, but chips of bone and soot,
more akin to the gravel that lines a country road
than the soft powdering you see in after-school specials,
where the young bury the old and are moved to tears
that leave their faces wet with the possibility of inheritance.

But ten minutes before the sun goes down
in this Texas border town, there's no time for crying,
and the river doesn't mince words, saying only:
Do what you must, just do it while I can still see.
So belly down on the rough rocks that skirt the Rio Grande,
I say goodbye to the old man with a bottle of Bushmill's,
a handful of buckshot, and a bag of Dixie Crystals sugar,
thinking I can vanquish him with a stiff drink, a good shot,
and something to make him come back sweeter.

~

Stop me before I make it pretty, before I get away
with it again. The truth is uglier than the ash
of my father, that stubborn additive that refuses to mix
with the current, to release me from this moment.
The dust that is the last of him sits on the river's surface,
so still that suddenly I want to take him back,
gold-pan him from the water the same way I try to distill
meaning from my childhood spent at target ranges,
firing at the black-and-white outlines of generic souls.

What was his one grand lesson? That you kill a man
the exact same way you love him, hit both head and heart
with the same round of lead?

~

The country poor used to mark graves
with their best piece of china—chipped bowl,
butter dish—too broke for even the smallest stone tribute.
They set a table at the foot of the dead and never came back.
When her son died, my aunt pulled her heart from her chest
like a dish from the cupboard, saying to the ghost of him,
"Here, eat and drink from me. I will feed you my life
while I live off the good bread of memory."
That's my translation of course, of the days I saw her
wander the house, holding his hairbrush to her face,
catching the last scent of him.

~

Here's what could not be reported earlier—
when you kneel at the mouth of the river
and feed it the ash of your father, something inside you
gives way, and that moment is the pretty twin
of the time he took the turkey gun and aimed
at his own chest, knowing that even a small bullet
can seize the heart. Until you lay him here
and learn to walk away.

Gun Country

There's a gun rack in the back of every pickup on the road,
children dressed in camouflage to welcome me back home.

I thought that when I left here, I was gone for good: pedal to metal,
tire to gravel, raising a flag of dust to wave goodbye.

But all roads lead back to these fields, where nothing stays dead,
and I stand again in a shoulder-wide stance, ready to plant

a slug for every year that you've been gone. What's a decade?
Just spare change to the heart. There's no cure for the ache

that is the loss of you; and the only comfort left is polishing brass,
measuring powder, sealing each cartridge with the blunt kiss of lead.

When I shoot now, I do it for the report sounding high
above the fields, for the echo that is the only answer that you give.

I do it to get close to you, that moment when you slipped off
the safety, put your finger on the trigger, and trembled at the thought.

The Dark-Light of Spring

I.

The stars were once just a handful
of rock salt on the black ice of the drive,
but my father had a need

for his sons to know major from minor,
pattern from mess. So we stayed the course
of winter nights, parroting the words he gave:

Cancer, Gemini, Cassiopeia.
The fog of his breath rolling over us:
Big Dipper, Little Dipper, Belt of Orion.

That year in school I learned mnemonic devices,
how the constellations were yarns once spun
to determine direction, when to reap or to sow,

and my father came home
each night to a tale all his own:
La-Z-Boy, meatloaf, vodka martini.

My mother faded to background
in the heat of his light. This was months
before the supernova of divorce

eclipsed all of us, and the universe cooled
to a spring in which I helped my brother
tape a glow-in-the-dark map

of the night sky to his wall.
That's when we learned to pull tight
the curtains and turn off the lights.

With enough ambition, any day could be
made dark, any sky could tell you the story
you needed most to hear.

II.

Two years ago, the undertaker shook my hand
        and said, "Mourning is a romance

in reverse"—I still can't get my mind
        around it, but I know he's dead-

on right. As my father lay hands folded
        in a pinstripe suit, I never loved him more,

that man who used to chase me around
        the house, the belt still warm from his waist.

Now his face runs alongside ads
        for backhoe rentals and used pickups

in the memoriam my uncle has placed
        in a local rag, turned into bookmarks,

and sent to my brother and me, as if
        we don't already mark our place

by where he used to be, chart our course
        by the North Star of the bullet

he fired through his heart
       ten years ago today.

Anniversaries keep track of us
       as much as we do of them.

Each year another plot point,
       another thumbtack on the map

showing where we've been since
       those funeral days when strangers

held us close, apologized for our loss,
       as they struggled to anchor

letter to letter, word to sentence,
       to forge their way like each of us must

to say something, anything,
       when nothing is enough.

III.

That day we entered the house
       of our father, we did so
              as strangers—

no key in hand or under mat,
       the door left open by police—
              and the first thing we saw

was a bullet hole through the family
       room wall. We crossed over then
             into another world,

went cartoon as the fat wallop of bat
    made contact with skull,
        stars circling round,

our inheritance, a disordered sky.
    What to make of it?
        For his part, my brother turned

each trash can out for what
    it could reveal, as I pressed my face
        against the blast hole

and stared into our father's room:
    magazines on the nightstand
        in even rows, the bed

so neatly made. In the aftermath,
    everything was evidence,
        sorted into piles

of keep or pitch, save or throw.
    We worked in silence,
        dumping drawers

into Glad bags and stacking them
    on the porch, where we collected
        ourselves at dusk.

It was only then we realized
    we'd spent all day in failing
        light,

never turned on a single lamp,
    the whole house counting down
        to the same black

of the plastic pooled at our feet.
       As we stared out across the corn,
          the sun stoked

its last coal and my brother brought
       the visor of his hand
          to his brow. Instinctively,

I did the same, as if we could see
       how close we were
          to him, how far.

IV.

My brother is calling because I'm the only one who knows
       how this week opens and closes, bound by the sturdy
hinge of loss that never wears thin. Our father is dead

another year and what is there to do but go on
       making small talk about what we've heard from home:
the sickness and health, the impending demolition.

Seems the vote came in, the word came down, and the old
       department store is next. The only class
that factory town ever had will soon be dust—

engineers are already calculating how each wall will give,
       ten floors fall next Sunday afternoon.
When the coast is clear, the urge to grieve will be followed

by the impulse to forget. One day soon,
       the empty spot on the skyline will mean nothing
to the newly arrived. So it is with mourning.

No one knows we're missing him until we say it.
Friends apologize. Strangers buy us a drink.
Each kindness is a depth charge

sounding out the limits of the space he used to hold.
As always, what is not said is more
important than what is. The store to be demolished

is the same one where our father bought us our first suits,
led us through the ritual of tailoring, the magic
of a stranger making something from our measurements,

all so we could be confirmed in a church
that never really fit—their heaven too small a place
in comparison to sky. In Brooklyn it's already dark,

and though they're hardly visible to the naked eye,
my brother says he can still make out the twins of Gemini.
An old story but one my father loved: Castor and Pollux,

one brother so unable to live without the other
that their father placed them side by side in sky.
What he didn't share was this: the truth about stars

in the truth about men. Brothers. Us.
You can draw a line between two bodies
in ink or blood, but that doesn't bring them any closer

together. Proximity can be a trick of the light, intimacy
an ever-fluxing span. Still, when we hang up,
he says he loves me with the same stilted voice

my father got each time he said goodbye—
a small and sudden comfort, that certain words
still turn a man all thumbs. As sure as salt, as stars.

V.

The wind took the last of him long ago,
but dead fathers make for stubborn ghosts,
and ours is no exception.

The first year I couldn't cry
or drink fast enough to kill what was
left of him. And now I pull out his things

just to put them away, unable to summon
him from wreckage: his belt and wallet,
a few service medallions.

Only when I'm half-asleep
can I come close
to assembling his face.

"Horseshoes and hand grenades,"
my father always said, meaning "close
but no cigar." Clichés were his home

remedy. "If it don't kill you . . ." his favorite
cure-all, sermon on the mount.
One lesson he didn't teach:

if you rub too hard at the last remains
of sleep or tears, a galaxy will blossom
underneath your lids—dark-light they call it,

the neural white noise of the eye,
twin skies that contain the only stars
I can convince to form the lines

of his forehead, his Coke-bottle glasses.
Still, certain features refuse
to be drawn—the frown

of his moustache,
his work-worn hands.
Some stories can't be told in stars,

each detail a too-distant light
that must be magnified
under the lens of memory,

which only gives
in equal proportion
to what it takes away.

II.

We've hung late in the bars like bats
kissed goodnight at the stoplights
—did you think I wore this city without pain?
did you think I had no family?

—ADRIENNE RICH

Bel Canto for Beginners

A quick slip of the paring knife and I'm behind
      the triage curtain, surrounded by the antiseptic
blue of tampon ads—sheets and drapes and bedpans—
      all the blue that wants to understudy blood.

A woman two drapes down is practicing
      her scales. Her voice chills the air with opera,
a throat gone florid with coloratura,
      glottis laid wide open.

My first love was a tenor who sang only my name,
      stretching those two syllables to their breaking
until his mentor told him, "Right now,
      someone else is practicing—and *he* will win."

He made a sign of it and hung it in his room.
      How many nights my eyes spied that sentence
from his bed. It was only a matter of time
      until he wrote another.

The nurse appears from behind the scrim
      that separates emergencies, doesn't bother
with gloves, just grabs my hand and pulls
      the flesh apart. Once again the blood begins

as the diva next door gives herself
      to full-fledged aria, and I imagine the small O
of her mouth, opened to permit a lone fingertip—
      the lips should never give too much away.

Hymn

It's only been an hour
and already someone has placed
Diana's photo above the bar;
someone else has filled a pilsner
with the ivory flare of a lily.

I'm always amazed at the speed
with which we make something
beautiful—if Ross were here, he'd say:
"That's what we do, Dear. Some boys
shoot things; we dress windows."

Once, in a time of plague,
a man painted his ceiling
the same deep blue of his lost friend's eyes,
thinking that a second coat
could make a sky to hold him.

"Say, Hon," calls Patricia, "say, Joey,
let's tie one on for the old girl,
crack open the Turning Leaf and toast
our little princess. In a world of queens,
she always knew her place."

Sammy laughs, lights a line of votives,
and the dim room is revealed:
the black paint has been touched up,
the bartender is crying. Quietly,

people start to leave; there are rules
about these things.

Some walk home in twos and threes.
Some go it alone for the first time in years,
listen to a sad song, go to bed early.
I stay until I am alone with him,
and while he cries, I lift the chairs,
hang the glasses, polish the difficult chrome.

Catching a Stranger's Eye during the Changing of the Guard

If only the Queen knew what goes on
underneath her nose and view. In the midst

of pomp and circumstance, a mere glance
can change the day. Take this fine boy

who just appeared outside the gates.
Even in the overcast light of London,

his eyes are two blue yeses. He smiles
and I smile back, mirror the tap of his finger

on the iron. This little code that shows
we know how one man can relieve another

of his stance. Just ask the others
in their silly hats. But oh, those reds

they wear, so much like this boy's dyed hair,
the unwavering, unnatural flame of it—

what a lovely way to burn.

Origami Heart

First, a ring from nothing
but a dollar bill and dime, spare change
set in pleats of green.

Then Easter lilies from cocktail napkins,
swans from movie stubs.
I should have known right there

he would bring the fever
of his hands to my every crook
and crease—bend of elbow,

back of knee—until I gave,
buckled into a fold, the flesh turning
ornament, the body a gift.

Loving the Haberdasher

He always wrapped his finery in tissue
with the same precision he undressed you,

folded your undershirt and placed it
gingerly on the bed.

With the lights off, it was easy
to mistake his care for detail with one for you.

What cannot be said, can be felt—
each silence between two people

teased into fabric and pressed
into form with the hard kiss

of steam. He taught you this. And how
to stand in front of the mirror,

fingering the fedora he left behind
in a way that reminds you what he gave you,

what he couldn't—a tipped hat
says both hello and goodbye.

Letter, January

It's that time of year when the young men in the village sculpt
the ones they pine for out of ice. Late last night, I heard them
with their mallets and picks, chiseling away at the face of love
while I tossed and turned. Today, as I walked past the statuary,
my arm turned suddenly warm—that silly spot of skin
you used to hold still thinks you're here.

At sundown, the lucky gals who'd been wooed
did a slow dance around their frosty twins, signaling to all
that they accepted this cold advance. But it was the others
whom I doted on, the unlucky boys who stood alone in falling temps.
When their would-be beloveds didn't show, the men left
their work to waste, each figure growing thin as desire must
when it's not returned.

At my window, well past midnight, I watch the abandoned
courtyard turn to slush; someone has sprinkled each monument
with salt. There is the young librarian, her small hands now smaller,
the book they once held now gone. The moonlight shines on her
wet face and . . . well, it seems everyone is crying.

Remember the first night you walked me home?
How the streetlights hit the fallen rain-soaked leaves
till the avenue looked as if it were strewn with pennies,
paving a road of luck we could have walked down,
if the sun had not risen on another day, the street
in need of cleaning.

At The Rhinestone Bullet

It's not church or therapy. Just a drag
bar on a side street you'd never drive down
where we gather at the altar
of country queens and false eyelashes

to forget the broken hearts and bills
waiting on the fridge, to play some Dolly
and practice her spell of glamour
with Max Factor and Jack Daniels.

Here, when you do a shot, you throw it
straight back, then knock the glass twice
against the bar, the first for the living,
the second for the dead.

When I miss her, I dab foundation,
brush loose powder until the blushing peach
of my mother's cheek becomes my own,
and I remember those mornings:

a working girl at the mirror,
Bonnie Bell and black coffee at her side—
in a man's world, a pretty face
is the best weapon you can carry.

My father used to steal her nail polish
to paint the sights of his handguns,
a drop of Jungle Red made it easier
to lock the target, make the kill.

At The Rhinestone Bullet, we shoot looks
equal parts fire and ice as we raise
our glasses, lower expectations,
and relearn the same lesson

we'll forget tomorrow—
there's no sorrow you can't kill
if you've got the brains to load your own,
the balls to pull the trigger.

At This Late Hour

Soon, the bottles you pour from will sing
  last call: half-empty glass on glass,
   JD hitting gin.

I wait for you, lose myself in news.
  Tonight, a man attacked his girlfriend
   on the lawn of her apartment,

sliced away at her while neighbors watched
  from picture windows. Only
   a twelve-year-old boy

with a baseball bat came to her defense.
  But he never had a chance to act.
   Instead, cops arrived

and took the suspect down
  with round after round of ammo.
   The boy is speaking

to a reporter live from the scene:
  I saw the sparks in the night.
   His words become sound bite.

Close up on his face, then cut
  to the aluminum sheen of bat,
   another silver lining found

as a woman's body is bagged
  in plastic, and you walk in the door
   with a kiss and a sigh for me.

You don't want to hear it—*please* you say,
    pressing your lips to my forehead.
        We unwind, watch TV.

The History Channel reports casualties
    are to be expected in the construction
        of any bridge:

the Golden Gate took eleven men's lives,
    the Mackinac holds twelve in its cement,
        the price we pay

for making two shores touch.
    You lay your head on my chest
        and fall asleep, while I stare deep

into the ceiling's makeshift universe,
    phosphorescent stars adhered years ago
        by God knows who,

the room full of unknown
    constellations. What patterns
        can be found that can help us

when we rise to routine, the same
    cereal from the same bowl, both of us
        uneasy, sick with luck?

Understory

With the lights out and the shades drawn,
it's easier to talk of these things—
the parents who beat you, the man who pimped you,
the emptiness you feel in your gut.

There's nothing but pitch black and the sound
of the trolley cable running underground,
the long drags of breath you take
before you start again.

Now is the time when most would say they're sorry,
give a kiss goodnight, but I know that this is how
two fucked-up men get to know each other,
showing scars without bravado.

In the morning, I'll start the coffee, put bacon on to fry.
I'll scramble the eggs. I'll butter the toast.
I'll make too much because it's all I can do
to keep myself from crying.

Earthquake Weather

"Earthquake weather," the locals mumble and grab another
cool one from the fridge. "If you end up staying, you'll learn
to read the signs," Rigo says, uncaps his longneck,
takes a swill. He won't say much more tonight—and you—
you've never told me the one thing I most need to hear.

Truth is, it's not that I can't read the signs,
but that I'm too scared to tell you what they say.
I've loved you to a fault for which there is no name
or measure, and we build upon it night after night.
Go ahead, pass out. I'll hold you as I always do.

By the dim light of the alarm clock and through the haze
of the night's cocktails, shapes shift: the coat rack
becomes a streetlamp, your mother's photo,
a girl I saw on the bus. She ran into an old friend
from rehab who wanted to connect.

But the girl just yanked her sleeve to show her tracks
and said, "You don't want to find me," her hand out-
stretched and trembling. She got off two stops later,
but still my mind runs the rail of her thin arm,
as if I can find the fault line that lies hidden in us all—

the ability we have to love and love completely
the thing that kills us best. Maybe Rigo's right.
Maybe if I stay long enough, stand still enough

underneath the doorjamb, I'll learn to read the jagged hand
of the seismograph before it signs our fate.

So far all I know is that a fear of endings
always blinds us to the beauty in destruction,
to that moment in the dreck when a girl wakes to sirens,
and in all the fuss of this shaking, shaking world,
her hands seem finally still.

Notes on Drowning

Another day of waiting for the pills to find you here
        and lift your spirits. I see myself in the collapse

of your body: age seven, a final exam in Swimming One,
        the twenty-foot deep end.

As I gathered my courage, the instructor gave
        an unexpected shove, and I fell into the pool.

I was supposed to dog paddle to the other side.
        Instead, I hit rock bottom

where I found a counter sky—one that I could touch.
        The smooth tile felt right against my chest

and calmed me, my mouth full open to the chlorinated rush.
        When the metal pole appeared to fish me out,

I wanted only to be left. But my hands took hold,
        and I was hauled back into this world.

The first thing you say today is that part of you is dying.
        Let it. There will be many drownings,

and for each you leave something at the bottom.
        And for each you learn a new way to breathe.

Assisted Living

"When you write about this, and I know you will, be kind,"
Matthew says, batting his lashes, doing his best
Deborah Kerr. But the phrasing is off, his voice slurred

with meds. For hours I've watched him remake an Easter
bouquet in a hospital pitcher. It's maddening, the many
ways those stems can lean as if they can't decide

how to hold each other. "Don't even think about it,"
he says. "The world doesn't need another poem
about flowers." I used to think these barbs

were how we fought *it* off, but now I'm not so sure
I know what that little pronoun is hiding.
It's easier to talk trash than to tell the truth:

the first time I saw him hit himself, my voice
was more a laugh than a cry, so surprised was I
that the body would catch its own left hook.

That night I was all cliché, holding a ribeye
to his swollen cheek as we sat watching bad TV.
Only The Home Shopping Network calmed him,

seeing the schlock that people bought if given enough
adjectives and a limited time, how quickly those who
could never hope for diamonds settled for Diamonelles.

The doctor arrives and reads his cue card for today:
"We'll have to wait and see if the positive symptoms
persist." He means the voices—the ones that told Matt to cut

himself, to run into traffic—now even they are good.
We hide the darkest truth in jargon. The psych ward
has been renamed The Center for Mental Health Services,

where patients are now "guests." And the dope they dole out?
"Mood stabilizers." The Doc leaves and we assume the best,
then the position: Matt's head curled into my lap,

while we watch another hour of Imposter Gems,
watch the clock tick down to the last chance for cultured pearls
and the end of visiting hours. Even the tulips are closing

up shop, except one that wants to open further.
When Matt goes to touch it, the tremor in his hand
makes the petals fall. "You should get out of here," he says,

"before I get a reputation." "It's far too late for that,"
I answer, and we laugh our secret laugh. I grab
his hand and hold it until his shaking is my own.

For Those Who Cannot Make the Journey

A woman is dying, a matter of days.
And what can neighbors do
but bring her small indulgences?

Plates of veal, of lamb
dressed in mint and rosemary. "Lovely,"
she says, and "Pass the wine."

We talk weather, she talks probate,
and how much you tip the gardener,
until the only thing left to do is dishes.

We try our best, but nothing can keep
her from the sink, now that every odd job
is another goodbye.

Instead, she wants us to be her eyes,
to help her see the city from the rooftop
because she cannot brave the flights.

"Climb the stairs," she says,
"and call it down to me." We don't want to
leave her but can't refuse.

So we ascend, and in voices
not quite our own, call down the halos of fog
around the bridge lights, the scent of smoke

from the chimney next-door, the steam
of our breath, the shiver of wind,
call down the full, buff moon.

Color Theory

"I envy your yard," an old woman once said,
leaning over the fence we shared, pointing out
a cardinal and a jay. "They seldom coexist,"

she told me in the quiet voice of the lonely.
"If you have cardinals, you can get robins.
Just nail a half an orange to the side of a tree."

And though I was young enough to want everything
I did not have, I never sliced that orange,
never nailed it to a tree. They stay with me still,

the things I did not do, the birds I did not call
with that proud color which refuses rhyme.
I've held sorrow closer than I had back then,

joy too. I know now how rare it is to see
those colors come to rest side-by-side—
the red breast, the blue.

Results

Under the fluorescent lights
of the city clinic, I can feel myself
becoming myth

as the counselor shakes my hand,
sends me on my way. I resist
the urge to look back,

think of the most beautiful
of losers—Lot's wife
in her dress of salt.

Instead, I walk in slo-mo
through the early dusk
of daylight savings,

join the owls in asking
the only question that they know.
My worst fear has come true,

and there's no one else to blame.
My worst fear has come true,
and I am still here walking.

Even with the sun gone,
some things won't surrender—
the blossoms of the Angel

Trumpet Tree remain open,
listening to a story
they've already heard.

Harm's Way

I've brought you here, to the base of the great tower
where you can see the two bridges that hold this city
and imagine the places they might take you,
because I believe in staging and the prop of the moon.

Because I want this evening to be aria,
the eye of the storm where the lead actor turns
to face the crowd and comes clean with what he knows.
But sometimes there's no music in the truth.

Especially right now, with me about to break
your heart and possibly my own. Soon, certain words
will turn me into cell counts, the roulette wheel
of the centrifuge spinning quietly in your head.

So I stall with small talk: how the tower was built
for those who fought the flames of the great quake.
Now tourists pay ten bucks a head for a view
those firemen never saw. I rail on

until you place your hand against my chest,
the same spot my mother always touched
every time she slammed the brakes,
her arm flying out to hold me back,

no matter the seatbelt around my waist.
"I never think," she always said. "My arm just goes . . . ,"
her voice trailing off into a quiet where the best part
of us resides. Some sentences cannot be finished;

others can barely be started. As I say the words,
I am steeled for the way that your eyes widen,
your lips part, and your jaw goes slack.
But for all of my rehearsal, I never thought you might,

in the shadow of the monument that honors
those who perished, take my face in your hands
and reclaim me with a kiss, as houselights
in the distance darken one by one.

Watching the Virus Attack a Cell

Tell me again why you want me
to see this—the virus that makes itself
again and again in my blood. Give me
the cold reserve of your language:

attachment, binding, fusion.
You mean to help me understand
how something replicates, loves
itself enough to make more of itself.

When I see the virus
press itself against the host,
I want to hate it with all of me
it hasn't got, but I see you—

and me—in its determined pace.
You with your method and me
with my need to know the meaning
of every word you give me:

*integrase, protease, reverse
transcriptase.* There's beauty here
if you can bear to see it. Look,
how one puts a little of itself

inside the other and soon they are
inseparable. Are we not the same?
Don't we corrupt each other, begin to look
a little like those whom we love best?

You don't think I get it, but I've got this
in spades. I know this body, how it has been

held and let go of. I know infection
is just a beginning, a kiss

that leads to another, more ardent kiss.
I know that when lips part,
when a virus buds, a sadness splits
into what must be another sadness.

But sweetheart, what's the use
of close work if it blinds you to the joys
that thrive inside us? Once, I thought
each of us to be a word,

and now I see that we are even less,
lone syllables—one useless
without the next. I am right here
beside you, prefix to root,

root to suffix. Come let us make
a beautiful sound together
that grows bigger, goes viral
each time it is said.

Sickness & Health

That was the season of blood draws and bad news,
the season I played Persephone seven shows a week,
tearing at the pale roots, the ceiling made of dirt,
no closer to sky than to the reason I was taken.

Then your grin and apple-green martinis—
our first date and we were an improvisation
of hands and mouths, the call of your body
and the response of my own, anywhere:

the bar, the street, underneath the daffodils
of a stranger's window box, until I pulled away.
Behind each first kiss, first time, there is
a hesitation, and behind that, fear or fears.

A partial list for your consideration: my body,
my blood, my cum; your body, your blood, your cum;
the downward spiral of immune systems;
the bull market of viral loads.

Before you, my dreams were of exam rooms,
paper sheets, the powdered touch of latex gloves,
vials of my own blood. Before you, I often woke
to the sound of my teeth grinding themselves to root.

Persephone knows the drill, she picked a flower
and was taken down below the living. It's a story
of beauty, the want of beauty, and the price
that is paid for even the smallest of pleasures.

I am familiar with the literature
in waiting rooms: dogeared issues of *People*

that tell of celebrity tragedies, suburban tragedies,
occasionally the innocents who survive near-tragedies.

So much time to lose yourself in the glossy pages
of someone else's sorrow, while you wait,
while you wonder why Persephone chose that one
flower out of all the glade? I do not know

his name, the man who infected me. I know his smile
and lacquered hair, the curve of his back
underneath my hands. I know I asked the question,
he answered, and we made our way to bed.

The most beautiful flowering bulbs are often infected
by a virus that paints their petals with wild brushstrokes
of color. The catch is this: broken flowers deteriorate
until they cease to bloom at all.

When I first found out, I was so cold-cocked
by the shock I felt all husk, no bulb, no flower.
Even as the earth opened up, I never thought it would
be me who disappeared.

And then there is your story: twelve T-cells left,
E.R. admit, chronic pneumonia case. On a bed in the ICU,
your odds grew slim as your waist, skin blossoming
with lesions. You were the nightmare

that we'd forgotten, the tragedy we were told
didn't happen anymore. As saline drips fed you,
as ventilators breathed for you, you closed your eyes
and fell into that quiet that each of must one day brave.

Beneath each fading daffodil is the bud of next year's
flower. While antiretrovirals brought you back,
you learned the lesson of those blossoms,
of Persephone herself: how to root down

in both spring and fall, in sickness and in health.
For a heart is not broken, it is made
into something that at first we do not recognize—
another heart growing fast toward any joy it can.

In the March night air you kissed me,
and when I pulled away, you held tight.
My sickness was your own, my lips the only answer
to the question posed by yours.

On the corner of 14th and Market Street,
I knelt before you, because of you,
and you brought me the salt and the milk of you,
the honey and sweat and sick of you.

Then you stood me up and kissed me again,
and we passed the words back and forth in silence—
secret words of the underworld, of the days and nights
spent under the living, words of contagion and cum

and the last of my fear, the balm of words,
the succor of words, my mouth holding your tongue
and your mouth holding mine. And there was nothing
I could give you that you would not welcome as your own.

NOTES

The last line of "Catching a Stranger's Eye during the Changing of the Guard" comes from the song "Fever" written by Cooley & Davenport and originally performed by Miss Peggy Lee.

The brief quotation that begins section II of "The Dark-Light of Spring" is taken from Thomas Lynch's *The Undertaking: Life Studies from the Dismal Trade,* Penguin Publishers, 1998.